This Paris Adventure Book belongs to:

Date of adventure:

Our favourite Paris memories:

ISBN/EAN: 9789082464726
Paris, December 2016, 2nd edition
www.traveladventurebooks.com

SNOWY SNOW LEOPARD'S
PARIS ADVENTURE BOOK

JACOBINE DE ZWAAN

ILLUSTRATIONS: TATIANA VAN DER LINDEN

Snowy Snow Leopard lives in Paris
She is the star of the zoo
During the day she shows her tricks
During the night… no one has a clue!

When all the kids are fast asleep
Snowy sneaks out of her cage
All night she walks around Paris
And yes, this is all very strange

She begins to play with little boats
In a fancy flowery park
Why do the ducks quack so loudly?
Are they afraid of the dark?

She plays soccer in a vegetable garden
But kicks the ball too high
It's stuck in a tree, what to do?
Should she give gardening a try?

All the pastries in Paris are delicious
Yet this is Snowy's favorite place
Their raspberry cake is so yummy
And it leaves lipstick on her face!

What an amazing view!
Snowy loves the sparkly lights
And yet she also feels dizzy
Because she's afraid of heights...

Snowy hops onto the merry-go-round
The old metro will start soon
She sings along with French songs
Hoping to share a happy tune

Snowy has a date with Carson Cat
On the stairs of a pretty street
He gives her a little kiss
Oh, Carson is so very sweet

In Rosa's dancing class
Snowy claps and touches her toe
But after spinning in pirouettes
She falls down like a big domino

Rosa
Bonheur

Snowy climbs onto a rooftop
She sits in between blue chimneys
Wait! What's that?
Is it a boat that she sees?

When Snowy plays with her balloon
She suddenly sees the sun rise
It's almost time to go back to the zoo
But not before eating a pizza slice

Snowy quickly jumps back in her cage
And covers herself with a wrap
She can’t wait to explore Paris again
But first she must take a looong nap…

The **Jardin des Plantes** is a large botanical garden with several nice museums. In *La Grande Galerie de l'Evolution* you can find beautifully stuffed animals that march over an African savannah. In the *Ménagerie* you can find real animals. The snow leopard is one of the star attractions of this little zoo. Don't forget to drink a glass of tea with baklava at the *Grande Mosquée de Paris* (across the street from *La Grande Galerie*).

There are many things to do at the **Jardin du Luxembourg**. There is a large playground (small fee) and kids can play with wooden sailboats in the basin. The classic puppet theatre is also nice to visit (www.marionnettesduluxembourg.fr). During a hot summer day the Rosary is quite refreshing, since it has both a sandbox and a little peddling pool (opposite *Musée du Luxembourg*).

The **Jardin Catherine-Labouré** (29 Rue de Babylone) is a hidden gem. Behind a large wall you will find a garden full of vegetables and fruit trees. It's an ideal place for a picnic (including sandbox and playground). Order your coffee to go at *Café Coutume* (47 Rue de Babylone, including high chairs).

Paris is known for its excellent patisseries. One of our favourites is **A. Lacroix Patissier** (11 Quai de Montebello, opens at 11.00 AM), a French-American pastry-shop based on the left bank, with a fabulous view of the *Notre Dame*. The cafe (which offers high chairs, a little kids corner and baby facilities) serves amazing pastries, crumbles, macarons and quiches. It's a perfect place to escape the tourist crowds and to enjoy a light lunch or coffee break.

The **Tour Eiffel** is just magic, even for adults. The *Champ-de-Mars* is a perfect green area to enjoy the world's most famous landmark. Relax at one of the two playgrounds (opposite Rue Jean Carries) or enjoy the merry-go-round at café *La Bonbonnerie de Marie* (opposite Rue de Belgrade).

The most beautiful merry-go-round is to be found at **Parc Monceau** (including swings and a nice playground). This lovely park is a wonderful place to pass the day.

Climb the steps of **Montmartre** and enjoy Paris from up high. The neighbourhood is not particularly stroller friendly, but it's worth the adventure.

- Must-sees: *Le mur des je t'aime* (Place des Abbesses), *Le Passe Muraille* (Place Marcel Ayme) and *Place Dalida*
- Streets with nice restaurants: Rue Lepic (number 35 hosts crêperie *Lepic Assiette*), Rue des Abbesses and Rue des Trois Frères
- Typical Montmartrian terraces: *L'Eté en Pente Douce* (23 Rue Muller) and *Le Relais de la Butte* (12 Rue Ravignan)
- Playground: Square Marcel Bluestein (behind the *Sacré Coeur*)

Parc Buttes-Chaumont looks like a background décor of a fairy tale. You can find walking bridges, little streams, a lake and a chapel on a cliff. Despite the occasional steep path, it is easy to walk with a stroller. Don't forget to visit café *Rosa Bonheur*, where the atmosphere is always joyful (including high chairs and a little kid's corner).

The museums of Paris offer many activities for kids. Search on www.mamalovesparis.com for the latest expositions and children's activities. **Centre Pompidou** is always fun for kids. At the *Galerie des Enfants* they can explore using all their senses. Don't forget to visit the balconies to enjoy the view.

Canal Saint Martin is known from the French movie *Amélie*. The area around the canal is lively and full of nice restaurants and shops. When the weather is fine, it is a nice idea to order a pizza at *Pink Flamingo* (67 Rue Bichat). They give you a balloon when you order. When your pizza is ready, the server finds you by the balloon and brings the pizza to your spot near the canal.

JARDIN DU
LUXEMBOURG

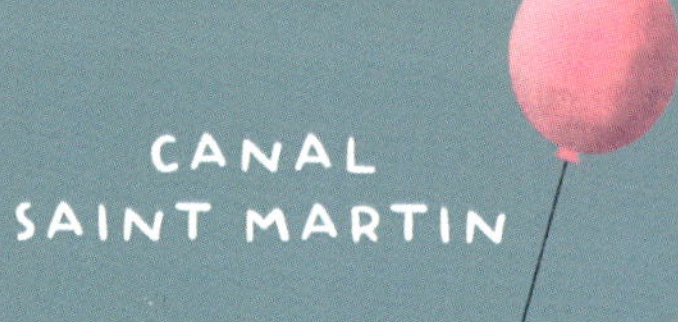

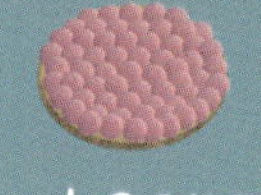

A. Lacroix
Patissier